BREAKING TOXIC

BREAKING TOXIC

*Love Yourself First,
It's Okay*

TONY D FLASH

Flash Supplements LLC

The content in this book should not be considered professional advice and is for informational purposes only. The content is not intended to be a substitute for professional advice. Always seek the advice of a related qualified professional if or when dealing with any related concerns.

Acknowledgments

A thanks goes first to the most high, I would not be able to do anything without God on my side. I would also like to thank my family for always supporting me no matter what I decide to do. Thanks to Vaughn Chiddick, Ashley Harris, Jenny C Rodriguez, Joseph Cole, and Jasmine Davies, all who read early drafts of the manuscript and provided vital feedback. Thanks also to my editors Cheyanne K. Gonzalez, author, and Kaylin Rodriguez, RN, whose editorial expertise, lively souls, and willingness to produce greatness helped greatly along the way. Thanks goes out to Erin Babb, whom I might say is one of the most dedicated creative directors I have met. I owe a great debt of gratitude as well, to all the people that sat with me and shared their story's; from doctors to police officers, I appreciate you all. I would like to thank Life itself! Life carries so many lessons as you grow spirituality and mentally.

GIVING THANKS

I would like to give thanks to the universe for allowing me to align myself with my true purpose. All energy matters, there is only perspective; my comprehension on what reality is has changed.

Reality is in the eye of the beholder. "I have no shoes; I am saddened by living bare foot. I have no feet; I am happy to be alive."

This quote replays in my mind frequently. When you begin to step into your truth, a shift takes place in your reality. While the shift is taking place, things start to change. The people, environments, and how you once saw the world, is no more. I am here to tell you that it is okay. Let go. Be who you want to be, living limited isn't an option. You should shine as life is written by you, and governed by the 'Most High'. Life is beautiful cherish the process. Be grateful, be full of color, be spontaneous. I am grateful for what I can offer to the universe. I am accepting of all life forces, the ones I can see and the ones that cannot be seen through the human eye but only felt through the human spirit. So, thank you universe.

Sincerely,
Tony D Flash

Contents

I

The World of Illusions

Wake up! Break toxicity, or it will consume you. You will come to understand that everything that is experienced in this realm is manipulated. The true currency of this realm is the "time" you put into doing things. When I look around, I notice that we humans live by 3 D's of life, and this is unfortunate. The 3 D's are DEADLOCK, DENIAL, and DEFENSIVENESS. We are in a deadlock when it comes to making better choices for ourselves. Even when the better choice has a shining light on it, we still ignore it. We feel it in our soul that the better choice is the one we should be making, However, somehow, we convince ourselves to take what seems like the easier route. Next is denial, one of our worst enemies. Denial is like facing the monster that you were afraid of as a child. Being honest with ourselves is something most people just will not do.

As "time" goes on and you grow, you learn that it was your mind playing tricks on you and all the while, the monster was not real. The enemy, the true monster, was YOU. All this time, you denied yourself of the truth by living in fear in exchange for what has felt like safety, and it is now the moment where this must stop. The person you see in mirror must rise both mentally and spiritually. You must break toxicity from where it starts, and it starts with you! This will feel like you are being attacked from the inside out and the only protection is who you are, and what you are, to yourself. Lastly, is defensiveness. Picture this to be an invisible cloth made of emotions that covers your logic. It is our body's' automated response to the lack of control we have within our circumstances. Defensiveness does not allow you to articulate clearly what you feel, and therefore you must BREAK TOXICITY with consistency.

2

The Truth Behind Our Lies

When you decide to understand the beings of this world, you must first understand the way they function. Philip Zimbardo, who is a famous psychologist, wrote a book called *The Lucifer Effect*. In one of the passages, Philip Zimbardo breaks down how there are neither good nor bad beings in the world. His statements and experiments went on to highlight some of the human behaviors. Human beings are caught in a systemic infinite loophole and they rarely take time to notice. You are probably saying to yourself "okay, how does this affect me and how will knowing this help me with breaking away from toxicity? No worries, in due time I will have answered your question.

You must understand thyself to understand how the world runs. The majority of the world's behavior is toxic in some form. Humans are accustomed to making choices that lead them to a toxic pathway. Human behaviors are repetitive and can change in situations based off a person's biases, emotions or what they feel they must do for survival. Making this kind of choices stem from what we choose to ignore in ourselves in attempt to gain a sense of relief and security. Allowing toxicity to flow in the mind without correction is like Zimbardo's Lucifer Effect. The Lucifer Effect emphasizes that even though we are solely responsible for our actions, depending on the environment we are in, we may change what we hear, see, and what we think. What we digest in the human brain is made up of our growth from our day-to-day experiences. Nevertheless, the true definition of the Lucifer Effect quoted from the text of Zimbardo is "a point in time when an ordinary, normal person first crosses the boundary between good and evil to engage in an evil action."

In my studies of toxic behavior, I have learned that utilizing the concept of the Lucifer Effect in analyzing my own behavior has shed some light on how toxic some of those behaviors actually were! Yes, I said it. You can contribute and partake in evil acts like the crossing over from good to evil in the Lucifer Effect. These acts can be detrimental to your wellbeing and can also be one of the highest forms of toxicity. Imagine cutting off your arm to use your other arm to grab a distant dollar, sounds crazy right? Well imagine being in a situation you know is bad for you but choosing to be there anyway. Understanding that these two are equivalent is the beginning to understanding toxicity at its best. Do not be caught up in your own Lucifer effect.

When you are out growing toxicity the world will reveal itself to you in ways you never saw before. There are people in this world that will sacrifice themselves to hurt you. While you are going through the transition of breaking toxic you must keep your eyes open, your ears listening, and your mind one with the heart. The heart, an organ we cannot live without, plays a great part in life that the five senses cannot see. Energy can be felt in different time zones when it comes to the matter of the heart. You can be millions of miles away and still feel the love someone has for you. If you can feel love from miles away, you must also be aware of negative emotions that can be felt as well, and you must become aware of the people of sacrifice.

The people of sacrifice are people who I consider the most destructible beings on the planet. The people of sacrifice are our darkest fears, our darkest thoughts, and our misery stuck in a time that only creates more misery. It is like being the earth and a tornado touches down, disastrous!

People of sacrifice are human beings who choose to sacrifice themselves, so another person can be destroyed in the process of their demise. All human beings are made up of the same matter, so I consider all of us to be one. If we are all one, then the mindset of the people of sacrifice is the mindset of us. When human beings try to sacrifice their wellbeing for your downfall, it is time for a re-evaluation. You must take a long look at yourself and even longer look at the person who is trying to harm you. They might be in a place where they refuse to rise to happiness, or they cannot get what they need or want. Perhaps someone they show interest in has no desire for them and continuously refuses their gesture, the bitterness begins to develop regardless of the situation at hand. Then it resonates deep inside them; this emotion can be extremely dangerous.

When someone has this notion of a great ego, usually malice follows behind. The damage that can take place if this is allowed can cause extensive backflow of toxicity. The overload can leave you physically or emotionally harmed depending on the level of stress. You might not notice at first what is happening, or you might think it is all bad luck, but it is not. Pay attention, energy is real and so are words of negativity. Both have the power to effect the atmosphere you live in and how you perceive your own environment. I want to remind you also, that it is your job to protect your energy and remember that even the people who are closest to you can cause toxicity. There are human beings in the world that would sacrifice themselves to see you fail. Toxicity has no limits when left unchecked.

3

The Lessons of Toxicity

In this chapter I will be sharing with you journeys that can shine light on what toxicity looks like. These are real life story's so that you can envision what you already deal with subconsciously. Bringing your experiences to the forefront of your mind is no easy task however, it can be done. You will be able to break toxic only once you are facing it.

Anonymous: "I was young and happy I had a best friend I called my sister; we did everything together. If she did not have it, I did. She would make funny comments about a few things we went through but, don't friends fight? We went to high school and college together and even got hired at the same firm. I got promoted to a higher position in the firm, and everything seemed to be going well for me. My friend on the other hand did not receive the same accomplishments and remained stagnant; what can I say, our work ethic was different. Nevertheless, I did not change on her. I did not go hang out with the higher paid grade colleagues and forget about her. I stayed solid with the person I came in this with. Our circle of friends started to change, and our money started to change but, I never changed on her. If she were short on cash for breakfast or lunch, I would still insist on handling the bill. One day I was walking by her office and I heard her say, "I would do anything to see her fail". I paid it no mind. I figured she was angry from work related issues, at least that is what I told myself. I used to see her around and my intuition would feel off, around her, but I brushed it off. Historically we would share pictures with each other, I mean like, woman stuff that was to stay between us. I would ask "like does this look good? What do you think of my body? "I can say I trusted her with such sensitive content. Despite the red flags that I noticed, everything else was great between us. No friendship is perfect, I said. So, months passed by, I am doing great, I am about to become the first female president of the company and suddenly, my world came crashing down on a beautiful Monday morning. At 8 o'clock my boss called me into his office. He pulled out his phone without saying a word and handed it to me. I was baffled. On his screen was a picture of me! I was naked! "Wow, the embarrassment", I screamed. "Oh My God! where did you get this from?", I asked. He calmy said "the internet." I immediately started crying. I said, "wait but, how?" He then went on to tell me how his wife received a picture of me and my best friend, and a message stating that we would deal with him in an inappropriate manner. I was so shocked and hurt, I could not believe what I was hearing. He didn't want to hear anything. I knew I was being let go. I worked my whole life for a career like this. What did I miss? I looked over my pictures realizing one thing, my friend had done a terrible thing to me. How could she!? I thought to myself. I had been nothing but good to her. Everything we ever did or spoke about was now public, or so I felt. I turned a blind eye to envy and words that I should have paid attention to. My best friend, my life. She hurt both of us! I went to question her confused and sad. I asked her "why?" She answered, "because I would rather sacrifice me and you both to see you hurt than to stay here and live underneath your shadow." I was shocked and could not believe what she was telling me. What did I miss? My whole life was ruined."

My response to the woman after listening to her unfortunate situation was "you were dealing with a person of sacrifice, you saw the signs and ignored them. You couldn't break toxic, you held on to the toxicity because of who they were in your life and what you deemed as the right thing to do." Many signs of toxicity were there for her to see. It was awful for her but, like most beings on this planet, toxic is only broken after you are.

In my travels to meet other people and explore how they dealt with toxicity I realized this was everyone's issue, the common denominator despite the numerator changing.

I spoke to a friend of mine that I met in Tokyo and she said she would not mind sharing her point of view regarding "people of sacrifice". She realized she was dealing with a person of sacrifice after I spoke with her and identified who the "people of sacrifice" really are. At the time she did not call it that, but after further explanation of how human behavior can be repetitive, and how they can and will sacrifice themselves for what they think their greater good is, she recognized that she had dealt with a person of sacrifice in her own life. This is her experience.

Mrs. Anonymous #2: "After 3 years it was finally over. I finally decided I was tired of my relationship draining all that was left to who I was; I ended it.

After realizing I was dealing with a person of sacrifice who just wished to sabotage my life, I found myself still picking up phone calls and answering text messages, feeling the need to comfort the same person who had betrayed me, to let him know that everything was going to be okay and it wasn't the end of his life so he'd be able to move on.

One night he called me on the phone, sounding a little more emotional than the usual. After maybe 20 minutes of talking and explaining to him that we were better off this way, the phone hung up. The next day I received a call from his family stating he was in the hospital and he had gotten into a car accident. I knew he had no family close by and proceeded to be the first person at the hospital to check his status and report back to his family. He was all smiles when he finally came around to waking up and saw me standing there. I had found myself there almost every day and felt sick to my stomach as he took one day to spill his feelings. He told me he was not doing so good and wasn't happy with how we ended things, he wished he had met me with his different mindset he supposedly had now. He informed me he was drinking a lot and went out driving the night of the crash and remembered being on the phone with me before the accident. I put the two together as I remembered him being a little more emotional than usual and the phone hanging up the night before. I thought his phone died. I wanted to cry, as I started to feel a sense of responsibility creep on me. I realized I would've been the last person he spoke to. Guilt had started to swallow me. Then, I remembered. I do not want to be here. We're over. I have allowed him to ruin my life and now here I am everyday feeling bad because of an irresponsible, irrational decision he made. Typical. This wasn't new. There had been countless moments he made me stay out of guilt, out of feeling bad for decisions he had chosen, for the consequences that came with those decisions. I was done. I realized he was trying to continue the cycle as I sat in the hospital with him. He would go so far as to put himself in yet another self-destructive position just to keep me with him. With no thought of his family, with no care of his wellbeing, with only decisions to sacrifice it all, just so I would not leave him. I zoned out as he proceeded to tell me how much I meant to him and how he was going to show me something different when he got out from there. I've heard it all. Imagine a woman who had been dragged through the mud, beaten and bruised for 3 years, being told by the one who dragged her that they would clean her off and everything will be okay because they finally came to the growth moment where they decided they "weren't going to do it to her again." That woman would not be okay, she would not trust or believe that to be true, and she would not care about the abuser's realization because it came at the cost of herself. I was that woman. I stared at my abuser as he spoke about things he has changed or would change but, they would only be his fantasy. I never came back to the hospital after that day. I made a decision. I knew then and there I would no longer allow his sacrifices to become mine."

My response to my friend after she shared her story with me was that she was lucky. I called her lucky because, lucky she wasn't in the car that night with her abuser and lucky she wasn't self-destructing because of the manipulation that was trying to be used on her. I told her that people of sacrifice are the most dangerous people you can meet. If they are willing to sacrifice themselves to hurt you, then they cannot be trusted. These people are often very hurt.

Pain comes in different forms. Pain can be stagnant, constant, and engulfing. Pain can be a cycle of madness. Pain can be the definition of insanity, doing something over and over knowing you will get the same results. When you are breaking toxic take these stories and learn. I know you see the signs from the overheard conversation in the office, to the drunk phone call while driving. Trust in yourself and know that it is okay to walk away.

Verbal Contradiction

Everyone has goals to do better but everyone does not know that they are capable of accomplishing them. Toxicity is blinding, it is goo of the soul and goo of the eyes. Most people contradict their own goals whether it is consciously or subconsciously. For example, "I won't be able to make it without him", "I can't get another job, "I won't be a good mother", "I won't be a good father", "I won't reach my goals". These are verbal contradictions toward the goals of mostly every being on this planet. If these are not specific to someone or your circumstances, that is okay. The point is that everyone has a set of goals in this life that they would like to achieve. Once that goal is set, most will come up with verbal contradictions as to why they cannot achieve it. It is a vicious cycle. Human beings do not believe in, or they stop believing in themselves, because it is easier to deal with accepting failure. It is easier to go back on your word than go forward. We must stop this completely in order to break toxicity. Negativity shouldn't flow through your body. Verbal contradictories are toxicity. This toxic form of living in the subconsciously placed thoughts in our mind over time or, by

others and their stories must be overcome; it is not the truth; it is an illusion. You can't allow the contradictions to dictate your true manifestation of what you see for yourself. You must remove yourself mentally and then the physical will follow. You must not allow the sway of negativity to pull you to a toxic dump, you must break it.

Breaking toxic is realizing over and over where you are at mentally and understanding that you will not be there forever if, you apply yourself to your own growth.

We are engulfed in toxicity. We live in a cesspool of uncontrolled emotions and fear. It may be a physical place that you experience the most toxicity at such as your home or your workspace. It could also possibly be a mental space. You should allow yourself to know that this is called the cesspool of negativity.

You ever went swimming and enjoyed it? Imagine having your trunks sink back in the pool as you get out of the water or, your bathing suit top accidentally loosens up enough to show the world a peek of what's behind the bathing suit. The shame that comes behind it sucks. Now you think to yourself, the next time I go swimming I will wear a different set of trunks or a more secure bathing suit. In that moment, you realized what you did not want to continue to happen, so you thought about correcting it to ensure it does not happen again but, you never followed through. You continue to attend the same gathering at the pool and you continue to do the same thing every time. You either lose your trunks or your bathing suit top and you are ashamed every day because the private sections of your body are flashed. Every day you try to enjoy the swim ignoring that you haven't made a solution. Now others are gathering just to see you make the same mistakes you made getting out of the pool since day 1. Knowing that what you are doing can affect you negatively and still doing it, is a cesspool of negativity that you've adapted to over time. Even though the swim is good, since you did not correct your actions, you live it again and again. Because you like to swim you think it is okay, but it becomes a trait of toxicity and you must break that. Next time you think about things you like to do that isn't the best for you think about the nest pool of negativity out there think about what you are deliberately creating. The cesspool of negativity can only be that if you allow it to be.

Unicorn Effect

The best way to know your limit of confrontation is to write down what it is that bothers you with people you deal with daily. Yes, that means the people you come across the most. This could be your siblings or co-workers, even neighbors. Take your time to write down what bothers you, even if you must do one person at a time. Write down the event that bothered you and remember why it was so sensitive to you, try to understand why it disrupts your energy. This is the first step to avoid reaching your limit. If you can understand why you felt that way, then you can pinpoint how to deal with it so that it never happens again. You are in luck! It probably will happen again. I know insane, right? But as I said, humans have the tendency to repeat their actions.

You can take advantage of this sweet opportunity to get ahead of what is coming. When something is about to happen that can cause an effect that brings you to a negative light, you should take a second to think. You should take 20 seconds to be exact, to think about something that does not have to do with the situation, like unicorns roaming the earth. Now that sounds absurd, but the state of mind it will put you in will either make you laugh or take a second again to think, wow imagine that. The unicorn theory, a theory I practice with many people. A theory that I created to give your mind space to develop a different thought pattern. The unicorn theory is a theory of mind manipulation with energy manipulation. If you manipulate the mind, you manipulate the energy. When you come back from that 20 seconds of an absurd thought process, I guarantee the situation at hand will be dealt with differently. Now in this state of newfound focus, answer peacefully and change the confrontation to something you can walk away from while keeping your cool; that is breaking toxic.

Reversing Your Doubt

Telling your inner self, you are not worth it should be a no compliant area in your soul. Everyone is worth it.

What we need to understand is that toxic is from within. I know that it is around us, but you decide what you are around, and you decide what you take in. We spend most our time telling ourselves we cannot do this, or we cannot do that, when in all honesty our only limit is us! The mind is a beautiful place to explore. Don't you ever tell yourself you aren't worth it. Don't you ever develop a mentality where you tell yourself it has to be, when it doesn't.

Accepting less of what you deserve is toxic. Taking in things that hurt you on a daily is toxic. Loving yourself less than you should be, toxic. So, it is time now to break toxic.

4

The Culprit

Honesty to me is like a breath of fresh air. I think honesty is the root, honesty is what lives. Honesty can be a permanent solution for solving all matters of toxicity. When you lie to yourself you create a space where your options feel faint and your thoughts weary, but telling the truth is like roots to a tree. It is you who knows what is and what is not. It is you who sees through your eyes and feels through your heart. If you have an enormous tree and you chopped it down, the roots would be exposed, and that is how the tree dies. Our honesty is our form of "roots". It's in ourselves to dig through the muddiest of emotions to expose the roots of our problems and just like the tree dying after the roots are exposed, some of your toxicity will begin to die as well, enabling you to move forward how you would like to. Expose the roots, the tree dies. Expose the lies with honesty, the toxicity begins to die. So, if you lead with honesty to yourself, the problems of the mind will die. Honesty is a divine power; it is a pure spell that you put on yourself and others. Honesty comes from within and flows easily when you are comfortable with yourself and your surroundings.

Words are spelt and written down, words are used to hurt or uplift, words create invisible energy. So, you must watch what you put out there in the universe amongst the beings of the world. When we speak, we spell cast! Imagine having a great time with a close friend and he turns to you and says, "high five I am enjoying my time." Almost immediately you would high five him or her. In most cases, we comply with the request for a high five. Foreshadowing a response by utilization of the proper words to bring the outcome about, is what you call spell casting. The words did not have to be written but spoken into existence, the act of what was asked comes alive. We spell words and use words to get our point across, so when you're speaking it is good to be honest while also maintaining a hint of positivity in all that you say. Remember, you are using the same energy on yourself as you put forth into the universe. Because what you put out will come back to you, it is best to watch what spell you're putting on yourself as well as on to others. The lack of honesty is a bad spell that will come back and bite you in the rear.

You would think this concept of honesty would be simple,

but it is not. It is also easy to define; honesty is simply put, telling the truth. Although over simplified, we are not always honest beings. Now, take into consideration what happens when the truth becomes a matter of perception. What then happens to the word honesty?

The origin of a person's "honesty" is very often forgotten to be understood as a form of perception, and because of this most of us have been deemed a liar in another's eyes, and that is neither wrong nor right.

The issue arises with the word "truth" in that what is true to someone can be altered. The best way to explain this is the common saying "there are three sides to a story," what they said happened, what I said happened, and what actually happened. Understanding that a person's truth is based off how they perceive the world is one of the most difficult things to do when it comes to breaking toxic. A task proven even more challenging, is to understand and acknowledge that most, if not all, of our own truth has been based off our biases from how we have grown to learn and understand the outside world around us.

We all hold preconceived views on how the world, and who or what, is living in it are supposed to operate. When an event happens that conflicts with what has settled in our core as "how it should be", we find ourselves at a cognitive halt. We are unable to fathom something is taking place opposite of what we know and hold to be true, can exist. This is where we will often find that "what actually happened" now conflicts with "what I said happened" and or "what they said happened". This cognitive halt brings with it our inability to listen and to observe untainted and openly to the experiences of others, and even of our own. If you cannot listen and observe, you can never understand what is really taking place in front of you; therefore, you must be truly honest to yourself on what you need to do, not what you want but, what you need.

On your journey to breaking toxic and being honest with yourself it would help to think of the world as an art gallery. The events that take place in this world are displayed pieces of artwork, and our experiences in it, the spectator. The artwork never changes its form, for it is as it always was. The spectator can only interpret the piece. They cannot change the pieces properties once it has been put on display.

In order to be truly honest, you must be able to tell yourself "the truth" and not solely "your truth". In order to truly be honest with yourself in this world you need to be able to tell facts free from the deceit. You must take a good look at yourself and say I will no longer lie to myself. You must be able to recognize that someone is giving you what is their honest truth and understand what that truth consists of. It will allow you to break away from someone else's toxicity when you understand yours.

What is honesty to me? You should always ask yourself that especially when you are alone.

When I look at honesty through my eyes, I see trials and tribulations of my soul. Honesty to me is always telling yourself "the truth" and not "your truth". Honesty to me is seeing 3 sides of the story. Honesty to me is understanding that everybody's opinion is right in their view. Honesty to me is listening before I speak and understanding. I see honesty as a picture painted from a person's point of view. I see honesty as someone's experience in the world. I see honesty as someone's lies in the world. I see honesty as an immediate action; the ego of a human being would call it brutality, roughness, a stop of calmness. Honesty breaks people's toxic. I see honesty as trust, to the people around you, to yourself, to strangers, to family, to your soul. It is right to be honest with yourself when you have started the healing process. Maintaining what you started with or gaining more is always the goal. Maintain your honesty to thyself while gaining more knowledge of thyself. You should not lie to yourself, ever. However, some things become our security blanket, those lies being one of the first security blankets we run to because some things are too deep, dark, and too tough to handle. Therefore, knowledge of thy self is the most important thing you can accomplish, because when you know yourself it is easier to be honest with yourself.

Now that you know and see what it takes to be consistent with yourself, what is honesty to you? Honesty is a major part of breaking toxic and if you do not know the truth you will always live the lie. Most of the time we know, so let's stop lying to ourselves and live honest so when toxicity places it's ugly face in front of us, disguised what we thought we wanted, we'll be able to tell that it's a lie.

5

Critical Choices

You must be a critical thinker, an adapter to life. You must lead by actions not just by words. A sentence without action is just a sentence. It comes into play when there is action. Thinking and acting on the better decisions to break toxic is a form of the law of attraction. Give yourself the mental space to continue to bring into your life what resonates in your heart. Give yourself the truth at all cost. It is important not to make decisions just off bare emotions. That can erupt into a chain reaction of negative outcomes that lead back to toxicity.

Write a goal down and read it every day. Put it as a screen saver. Your goal should state "I am breaking toxic and will be free from toxicity". Apply it to everything and you shall break toxicity. Be a critical thinker by always thinking of 6 outcomes. I call this the pentagram protection. You are in the middle of the star because you are the main lead. The circle around the star is the truth protecting you from the toxicity. The questions are the angles of the star.

The first outcome question that should pop into your head is, does this choice affect you in a toxic way? You should always be able to ask yourself that before, during, and after making a decision. It is a part of being a critical thinker and is also a part of the pentagram protection that must be followed in order for the process to work. You must really contemplate what it is that you are doing, think about what that person is doing, and decide your best move from there.

The second question is, "am I happy with the decision I made?" When beings of the universe ask themselves this question, they usually do not answer. Some may think it is easier that way, but it's not. Everything is a choice

Not making a decision, is making a decision. Self-reflection is a must if you are insistent on the betterment of yourself. When it comes time to make a decision, no matter big or small, and emotions fill your mental space, you should think to yourself "am I okay with this decision?". Ask yourself more than once "is this something I can see myself over coming?" Are you going to be able to look back and say it was worth the energy trade off or is it going to be a moment where you gave the main currency of the world, which is energy, away for free? If an immediate action is not in place, then what? The answer is you must mentally move forward so you can physically move forward. Life is like a game of chess. You must take every move seriously. The only difference is that life is not a game. In the world of alchemy, they teach that to make something, you must lose something. Nothing can be expected to be created, if nothing is being put into creating it. So, when you decide your future while your living in your present understand that everything costs something, even if it is charging you mentally.

The why is the power! The why is the power! The why is the power! Always ask yourself why? Why is the sky blue? Why is our blood red when it hits the air? Why does this affect me to where I cannot concentrate? Why do we live to die but die to live? Why do we sleep? The why is the power! Question what you seek and seek what you question. This must be something that is done without hesitation. This way of thinking should only be used as a tool to challenge your toxicity. It should not cloud your mind to where you can't think of a toxicity free life. It should be this questioning mentality that is developed in the early stages of changing.

Intuition is something that is in all of us. The feeling of butterflies is something we all felt or dealt with in some form. I call it the swirling energy. The feeling that comes in your body that cannot be explained is held in energy that is not processed correctly, there is no logical train of thought just bare emotions guiding you to the direction of your attraction. This causes physiologic responses like an increase in heart rate, funny feeling in your stomach, or the goose bumps with your hair standing tall on your body. That is the "swirling energy" using its techniques to gain a different source of your realization inside of you.

Meditate to alleviate! In order to gain control of your mind you must first go in it. You must understand yourself. Breaking toxic is breaking you. All your biggest fears are inside of who you are. Meditation is a great tool to calm the storm. This is a place you can inherit your truth just by taking 20 minutes out of your day closing your eyes and thinking. This is a different form of meditation I speak of. You usually hear people say "clear your mind" when they meditate but what I'm trying to do here is create a thought process in your mind that allows you to think outside the box, in a controlled state.

This form of meditation is like looking over your favorite foods or food you do not like and picking one to deal with. Singling out one thought at a time. I say fill your mind because it is already filled, just not with the right stuff. Trying to act like something is not there is trying to act like you cannot see when you have your full vision. Take your time to scroll through your mind. It is much more important than scrolling through your phone. Throw away the traits that bring you down or hold you in a place you do not want to be in. Take the good traits and add them to the new traits that you are learning to develop. You must alleviate the myth of having everything together at a certain time. IT IS NOT A SOLID WAY TO LIVE.

Consuming yourself with someone else's limitations can only harm you if you allow it to. You must set fourth good intentions from your heart. Toxicity is all around, but that does not mean you need to be engulfed in it. When you break toxic you will learn that part of loving yourself enough is to know what is and what is not. Conquer thyself in the gentlest way. Have you ever heard the saying your such a gentle giant? Well, that is what you need to be for your breakthrough. Understand that you are bigger than your toxicity!

The human in the mirror can hear you. Speak to yourself! I highly recommend you speak to yourself constantly. Say things out loud. You ever heard someone say something and you did not see anyone around. Well, it is kind of the same concept. Find an open space where there is no one there and speak out loud to hear your thoughts. If they give you the "what the hell?" feeling then, rethink them. If they make you feel toxic, then rethink it. Apply a different strategy when speaking to yourself. Speak as if it happened already. Always speak truth to yourself because you know your truth. The truth that is buried in the box inside of you. Open that up and allow it to speak to you. Look in the mirror when you feel like lying. After you do that ask yourself "is this the way that will help me break toxic?" If not, regroup your thoughts and apply what you have already learned. Always check the human in the mirror first.

Some choices matter considerably in helping us to acknowledge who we are. To ourselves and to other people. Some choices are not relevant. In everyday aspects we learn more and more about ourselves. We can make an absolute bad decision that may look to others that we are one way but, in making that mistake we learn where our own "personal line" not to cross is because of how it made us feel. Now we know more about who we really are than we previously did. Some people might use that action to define us. You are exactly who you are regardless of what you do is what they will say. That is okay, because toxicity is from within so try to understand, that person's pain is not your fault. Your actions will not change their projective behaviors or thought process either. Spend less time trying to show someone you changed and more time actually changing for the future you.

Change for you, while continuing down the path of eliminating toxicity. We all go through life with an idea about who we really are. Going deep into one's mind will eventually leave you all alone, at some point you will be faced with a choice. The choice of being free of toxicity or dealing with what you are tired of. It is like continuing to build a puzzle that is already finished. You do not need any extra pieces; you have it all in you already to make better decisions. When the better option is chosen it will unravel you. It will reveal what you have known for so long. You might come across situations in the past that you do not agree with or look back at the way you used to think and challenge it. The key is to understand that the image we have of ourselves in our head is not always the image we put out there.

When we act, we subject ourselves to a test. You start to ask yourself "is the vision of myself that I had inside my thoughts, a good vision?". If it is not, take action and recreate what you believe to be is a better vision for yourself. This is indeed necessary. When we have an idea of ourselves that does not match reality, we cause harm and trouble to not only ourselves but to the people around us. This action must happen over, and repeatedly because over time we change. It is important to break down and get rid of the things in our head about ourselves that are lies. We have to be persistent, because lying to ourselves is easy, but the long-term consequences of the lie can cause internal along with external damage. Then, you'll spend most of your life trying to heal what you think is broken. Nothing remains broken if you no longer want to be broken.

Are we defined by our choices? Or do our choices define us? Everything happens with a purpose. Your life is defined by the choices you make every day. Knowing your purpose empowers you to break away from toxicity and make better choices. Choices are important. If you surround yourself with negative energy you will become negative. "What defines you?" Is a frequent question that you should always answer for yourself. Be better than the foundation that you once knew. What has influenced you was it society? It may be society who you thought has molded you but, in reality, it was the actions you've taken which determine another human's mindset about you. Those actions came about because of the choices you have made, which in turn have an influence on our lives and on how people perceive us. You hurt someone, break their hearts, you will always be looked at as the bad guy to them. Keyword here is "them", you should not choose to empathize with this person because you feel guilty. That action can hold you back from releasing toxic energy. You do not live there anymore you are free, even if the other person is not. Imagine you are working out in the gym, you visualize yourself being in the best shape of your life as you are doing your workout, and there is another set left. You start telling yourself, "it's okay, you can do better tomorrow, "but the thing is, you can do better today! An inch moved forward is still moving forward. Toxicity leads to procrastination, which eventually shatters every dream you have had of having the "perfect" you.

Do not allow "them" to box you in. Do not give up, because every day above ground, is a good day. You must make that choice; you have to get serious about it or it will never happen. The day you start breaking toxicity everything in your life will fall into place. Personally, I started off indecisive, undetached, scared, and courageous, all at the same time. It is far from easy but worth the journey. Since I became honest with myself, I come off as I am to brutally honest to the world but, lying to myself is an old habit I will never pick back up. I do not allow old habits to separate new bonds. Deciding on what you want and who you want to be clears the way from unwanted realities. We live in a dream world. You are surrounded by illusions, and these illusions change when you change your thinking. Tell yourself you got this. Speak highly to yourself and of yourself. Say positive affirmations out loud. Eat. sleep, breathe it, and your life shall be transformed.

So, what defines you?

6

Choosing Your Light

Every being in the universe has a light inside of them. You can call it a soul, you can call it god, or intuition; you could even call it power. However, light is energy and energy is light, and we all have light inside of us. The light is a gift that never dims. Even during our last breath you are able to see the light when the body is empty as it transitions to a different form of energy that the naked eye cannot see when you die, and in that moment of passing, your body can feel it. It knows what's right for you while you are still awake in this world, and even in the next world. You must harness this light. Learn that it is the creator of your true self. Toxicity can lock the body up and also the mind, from which the light heavily shines through. This light we were born with is beautiful and everlasting. It is also infinite on an external and internal level. Find the light because it is the map to the rest of your life. This light can be used for "darkness "or what we deem as evil, or it can be used for good. The common light in which we all possess, can be put to use in many different forms or scenarios tailored to each person's circumstances. For example, a female tiger is known for her skillful hunting and aggressive behavior around her cubs. Her killer instinct makes her one of the best hunters there is in the animal kingdom. As she transitions from a fierce and dangerous fighter, to a loving, caring mother, it's interesting to observe her light being utilized in different circumstance she may find herself in. It has been documented before that this same tiger has been seen raising a lost baby gazelle, that it is also known to hunt. Basically, her natural instinct, which would be to love and care for her offspring or an offspring, is powered by her inside light. This natural instinct embedded in her allows her to switch from "hunter "to "caregiver". I shared this story of animal life because I believe it is more than necessary to understand the different forms of light but, to also understand that there is one light in all of us, and it can bring forth an abundance of awareness.

To achieve this awareness and to embrace your inside light, you must first acknowledge that it exists. You have to sit back and go in your mind to allow your soul to show you itself. Open the eyes that have no flesh. In the story with the tiger raising the gazelle, I showed you that your light can shine in different forms, and that you have control over it. Even though we grieve, we also cry, or we smile, and we also laugh. Our brains are so powerful that we can change the thought process in any moment.

Actors get paid for perception. They create a story in our mind by understanding the characters' mind and who they need to be, and how they need to feel in each scene While you're watching the movie, most of us find our selves being swayed or captured by the emotions of the characters in the movie without the thought of reality. In reality, there are cameras everywhere and an entire paid crew filming a paid actor to capture the audiences' attention. If you manipulate the mind, you manipulate the energy, and if you manipulate the energy, you can do anything. This is by far one of the most truthful statements in Breaking Toxic. You must have repetition, consistency, and determination determination to live a better life. It may not be done in a day, but the toxicity will be broken someday. Use your inside light to guide you to what you already know to be true, that is, happiness is from within and the only way toxic continues to happen is by you allowing your mind and energy to be persuaded by it. You control every aspect of your own feelings including the ones you think you do not control.

SYMPATHY, the word that travels in silence but kills out loud. The definition of sympathy is the feeling of pity and sorrow for someone else's misfortune. This word can be described as losing thyself. I believe sympathy plays a part in toxicity because, it allows you to feel and nurture to one's nature of stagnation, especially if you're on the receiving end of the wraith of sorrow. When breaking toxic, you must keep going. It is like a trick you play on yourself because you are accustomed to playing yourself for the lessor good.

In a workplace environment, I will describe to you how sympathy is toxic if you allow it to be. Say there is a job you do not like and every day you are looking for a way out, but you just haven't found it yet. You look in the papers to find that there are no openings for a new job that you like. There aren't any in the ads, or any online that make you happy either and this makes you unhappy. Now, you must continue working at the place you are dying to get out of. Bills have to get paid, right? Kids have to eat, right? Now we know why you are working there still. Let's fast foreword to mid-afternoon now.

In front of your desk your coworker comes over with the most heartfelt story on why he must leave and asks can you stay to finish his work. So, you buy into what he is saying and this leaves you at work longer than the usual. Now, fast forward. Week after week, after week, the same thing takes place but, because your coworker makes your eyes watery and makes your heart filled with emotions, you buy into it again and again, and again. Shame on you. This is the downfall of sympathy. You stay in circumstances you do not like, because you are swayed by your own emotions even though you know this is not the best way to break out of toxicity. When someone knows that you are easily influenced by emotions of the heart, sympathy can be used as a weapon.

In a relationship with a partner, it can render you paralyzed and paranoid by your own thoughts. It is like having bad cells in the body being produced from having bad eating habits. Yes, it is your cells that are creating more bad cells by you consuming foods that are not good for you. You have not given your pain and your needs the acknowledgment they deserve so that you can leave. In a relationship, someone can see that you are ready to leave and use every moment that you shared together that was positive, against you. This manipulation can alter the way you respond, your mind and your heart can fall into a place of confusion, by this time you'll assume the role of doubt. You'll convince yourself they care because they tell you they care, that's when the saying "actions speak louder than words" should play in your head. Fun fact, a person will be everything you ever wanted just to keep you right where they want you.

Manipulation through dialect is another way to trap your mind. We as human beings tend to give people test, while we already have the answers. It's a repetitive torture we inflict on ourselves. It isn't fair to the student that passes or wants to pass the "test", and in this case, the student that wants to pass is you. You want to move forward and not look back, you want to grow and have fun. This is why sympathy can cause or completely stop you from breaking toxic? What you would like to hear will be said, and what you want to see will be in front of your eyes. That is a distraction from you breaking toxic especially if it has been months, or years, and the result has remained the same. Most likely in a day or 3 it will not change. I am not saying you cannot be sympathetic to other human beings, but I am saying when being sympathetic turns into being taken advantage of, you have to have "truth time" and call it for what it is. If you never break that sympathetic cycle, you will remain in the same place. Yes, right where you never left. Understand the trials ahead. Put your best foot forward and challenge yourself. Tell yourself the change is a must and if you stay in toxicity, the cycle will continue. If there is a split between consciousness and the physical then you are torn between fake and real, realization of what is actually taking place is important. Your heart already left. Don't be caught up in sympathetic disaster.

When your light roars inside of you it is a sign. Everything will feel wrong inside of you even if it physically feels good or mentally creates a false healing space. Follow your muscle memory. If you hurt yourself before doing something physical, the body and mind remembers. That shock wave of pain will not only be remembered in the mind but, also in the body. Trust the process! You have to believe in yourself so that you can grow stronger. When you grow stronger so does your light inside and the guidance that it offers. Even though there are plenty lights all over the world and all over the universe, as a being of endless power, you are capable of putting blinds on when it comes to other being's light. Realize that you are in control of your light and your shine isn't any less significant than the next person's. You won't stare into someone else's' light again once you can feel yours, you won't have to be deceived by falsified lights. Do not get caught staring into someone else's light. That would be the equivalent to a deer getting caught in head lights, You'll want to steer clear of those situations.

Sometimes in these places in your mind, you go through a darkness that you cannot seem to understand. When you were born, you came from darkness and all you had was your mind. You could not see anything or really hear anything, because you were trapped inside your womb until you developed full term and had to evacuate your mother's belly. During that time, you were still developing who you were going to be, when you came out of the womb. Darkness is where you created yourself and now all these years later, you are scared of where you started from? The key is, you must control your mind while you visit the darkened area in your mind because this place will probably be full of sewage or in other words, toxicity. This can be frightening, I understand. It is frightening because although you are being brought to a place that you have the ability to control, you must navigate this area where the toxic situations or situations that brought you to the darkness in the first place, reside. But in that place, in the so called dark, you can create light, and you can create solutions. No one can follow you there, to this dark place, It is you that makes the darkness a dark place. From my experiences, the darkness is where you can recreate and rebuild yourself. This is where you started from, and the best part about starting over is that you now have experience on what not to do and guidance on what needs to be done; for your greater good, for your peace, it is your life, and you choose what thrives in it. My belief is this darkness we all fear, is light in a different form, it is misunderstood and scary because every time we go there it is a negative experience re-lived. Although this may be true, there are some forms of meditation that require you to close your eyes and clear your mind, that links you to inner peace where you'll be able to control your feelings. I know it's hard to meditate because the first thing you see is darkness when you close your eyes. Darkness is a platform for creation.

Whatever you want to envision can be created through a simple thought. This is your life; you have to live every second like your creating time. No one can truly teach you about your toxicity and the inner darkness where it is found. You have to see it, you have to feel it; you have to control it because you're living it.

7

Behind the Toxicity

Disclosure: The following chapter is based off real life people and their experiences in situations of toxicity. The in-

terviewees must stay private due to concerns of disciplinary action that could be taken by their jobs or for their safety with their partners.

Interview 1

Interviewer: "Hi, how are you?"

Interviewee 1: "I am okay, a little nervous to speak about the things I am going to speak about today."

Interviewer: "Can you tell me a little about yourself?"

Interviewee 1: "So, I am from Brooklyn, you know the GRIMEY city. I love me some grilled peanuts, hot and fresh peanuts, or that good ole jerk chicken being made by the Rasta mon on the corner on the fresh grill. Well, somewhat fresh but, it is still good. Dam I love that shit."

Interviewer: "What are some good traits or morals that you find to be the most helpful while dealing with toxicity?"

Interviewee 1: "Patience must be the most important trait I carry within myself. Patience with myself so I can make better choices or analyze the situation differently."

Interviewer: "Have you ever had a reality check, or moment of clarity in a situation? Can you tell me your story so we may analyze how your reality check came about in this "fake reality" we live in? "

Interviewee 1: "Of course I can. The first time I had a reality check in what I would call in a "fake reality" is when I could not protect my family. When I was younger, I grew up in the rough neighborhoods of Brooklyn. I will not say any place I do not want anyone to catch on that it's me speaking, but anyway, I joined a gang at a young age. I used to see them stick up for their people, I used to see them help with groceries with elderly and I used to see the family members of those gang members being well protected. Everyone knew who they were, what they were, and how to behave. It gave a sense of pride to say you came from them or belonged to the gang. It also gave a sense of religion, something like a cult. I used to walk into stores and say "hey, I'm so and so, from such and such, let me hold this for free," and the store owners would abide. I was so young at the time so there were so many things I didn't pay attention to. My mother used to yell at me like "I don't want them boys hanging around here it's not safe!" In my head I was like, no way. Still being a younger member of the gang, I was not involved in the deepest parts of it yet, so I did not see what the elders did. However, I was definitely being groomed by the gang to take on a greater role. As I got older, I started to see things and got deeper involved and that's when it hit me. That's when the truth and my reality shattered, that's when I experienced a reality check in my fake reality."

Interviewer: "What exactly did you experience during the moment you realized that this was a reality check? That sounds like a young, free to do whatever you want, type of life."

Interviewee 1: "Yea, I thought the same shit man. Wait can I curse? My fault. Okay, I am ready. I thought it was free but, everything came with a cost. For example, when they were sticking up for their people, it was because they made them pay for living in "their neighborhood" on top of paying rent and struggling, something I didn't learn until later on. When they were helping the elderly, they were trying to frighten them so they would never tell the police what is going on in their buildings or outside them. And when their family was protected it was because they were killing other families of other gang members or just the other gang members, and needed to protect their own, so they basically had security around them. I call that living scared. Everyone knew who they were in the neighborhood because not one person was not being affected by their actions. You would hear other kids speak about how they can't go somewhere because this gang made a claim to the territory like a school or building in an area and you'd technically be considered as being from that area. I didn't see it because I was a part of it. I didn't feel it because I was, I was... just living in a fake reality."

Interviewer: "So, when did the reality check begin to set in? Talk me through those emotions"

Interviewee 1: "When I lost my brother was when the reality began to set in; he was a neutral. A neutral is someone that is not in anything at all, gang wise. He was a great kid, had aspirations that could reach the sky. I do not think it set in until a couple years back when the anniversary for his death came around. I was drinking and made a toast and said I will always protect you, but I realized I already failed in that. I realized that my mother probably would never forgive me, I realized it was my fault. After I learned about all the true horrible things that were taking place, I told the gang I wanted out. So, they let me go, it was like a blessing. But what I learned later was, for one of their recruits, they told him to kill my brother to get in and he did. So, see, that was not the way to protect him or my family; that was not a way to live. It was a reality check in a fake reality because everything I was living was fake, his death was my check. Now I am grown and still do not have my brother."

Interviewer 1: "Sometimes what you think is right isn't. Toxicity comes in many forms and that's why you have to look with not just your eyes but with your heart and mind living together as one, and that's how you can break toxic before you even get down these roads of destruction. I feel that the protection you were looking for was based on a good place, but toxicity was what you found. A toxic environment, producing toxic behavior, manipulating a toxic mind."

Interview 2

Interviewer: "How are you feeling today?"

Interviewee 2:" I am feeling okay, just trying to take it one day at a time."

Interviewer: "What does reality mean to you?"

Interviewee 2: "Reality is what we live in, it's what we make up of this world. "

Interviewer: "Do you ever feel toxic?"

Interviewee 2: "I mean who is not? The habits we pick up come from the beginning, well that is what I think."

Interviewer: "Can you tell your story to analyze where you experience toxicity, bring us into your reality and perhaps speak on a moment in time you had a reality check in what I deem to be 'fake reality'?"

Interviewee 2: "I come from a family of doctors. So, I really did not have a choice on my profession, let us just say it was heavily geared to towards being a MD before I had any say in the matter. Basically, I attended a great school and of course I graduated as Valedictorian. I studied very hard. My reality check came when I started to compare my living situation with my happiness at work. My true reality was very different than the one I dreamed I would have. I could not have imagined I would be in this place at this time during my career. I am going to save lives, I said. I am going to have a great day, every day, people are always going to treat me well, and I will have piles of money, and a boat. This would be endless fun because it is something that all my family members do. Boy did I imagine wrong."

Interviewer: "So how do you feel about being an MD?"

Interviewee 2: "How do I feel? I feel that we are all human and the expectations of a doctor are held way too high. I get it, when you are sick you count on us, when you're happy you count on us, when you're mad you count on us. The reality is, sometimes we are not at our hundred percent and we are humans as well. I know a lot of people cherish us like Demi gods. We are not, we are just people who practiced harder in medicine than the average person. I do not mean to speak so low of my fellow MDs, but I know for a fact that if anyone put their mind to it, they can become one as well. I have a boat, but I never get to use it. I'm always working and even though I buy fancy materials, I still end up working even more. You ever ask yourself why your doctor is kind of old? He's still working to pay off school debt or he just finished school 5 years or 10 years back and he's still fresh in the medical world. How is it that they think you can take 1,000 years of medicine and place it in a 10-year experience? When you are an MD, People are not as nice to you as you think, they get mean when they get sick. They curse you out if you make one little mistake. You must live your life basically as a saint or you can get stripped of your license. I don't have piles of money laying everywhere. I struggle too. It might not be the struggle someone else deals with, but I had my share of hardships. There is a struggle to be dealt with on every level. It is not always fun and happiness. We have to be on the front line for every sickness, we have to give up all the "fun" young years and consume ourselves with learning to treat patients. We can't hide from sickness. My reality Check happened when my assumptions on what a doctor is supposed to be were shattered, it is hard, it is lonely at first from all the studying and it is lonely later on because of the constant work. The boat that I purchased might end up driving itself."

Interviewer: "I think it's crazy how you described what you feel is a reality check in a fake reality, most people would have never thought that these issues exist amongst doctors. You guys seem like you have everything under control, and you have it down packed. I guess in a reality of seeing you guys as perfect, we cannot see that. Some might go as far to say perfection doesn't exist. Situations when you think everything is going to go perfect can create a toxic way of thinking and can leave you blinded by looking at a scenario through rose colored glasses. Toxic situations are in every job title or career, but you have to either walk away or recreate a new view of life and way of being to implement what you truly want and break free of what is toxic.

Interview 3

Interviewer: "You look like you are glowing!"

Interviewee 3: "Yes, I am excited to talk about this part of my life!"

Interviewer: "Okay, let's get to it."

Interviewer: "Can you tell me a little about yourself and what it is like to be a woman cop? Also, I'd like to know, have you ever convinced yourself to accept a reality you didn't want?"

Interviewee 3: "So, I always wanted to be a police officer, the pride and the strength that it carries is very uplifting. I wanted my kids to have a great role model, someone they can look up to. I did not want to be the average stay at home mom. I was a superhero at home, and I wanted to be a superhero in the real world. That is what I thought of police officers. The coolest part is, I am the law enforcement and help citizens stay safe. I get to carry a gun all the time and in times of danger, I get to face it head on, and I am the one being called to the rescue. Training was difficult, but I got through it. I gained a couple pounds after but, hey, that is what it is if you are not walking all the time. I figured being a cop my kids would be protected by a bigger family than ours, they would be protected by the family of the government. I figured there could be no wrong; well, boy, was I wrong."

Interviewer: "What do you mean when you say you were wrong? What brought you to this realization and would you consider this to be a reality check?"

Interviewee 3: "There is a lot of pride in this job. I think that's why it's difficult for a woman to be a police officer. There are way more men than women, and if you do not see the stares coming from them (the men), you feel them. Imagine getting a creepy stare from a man in the morning, and then later on you're on your day tour with the same person that gave you that stare and find out they're also your partner.

Imagine always being caught in the middle of guy conversations that seem to be mostly sexual. Now at this time, I realized my kids still look at me as a superhero. I never needed this career for them to view me as such. I realized it drew more attention to them because I walk a line against crime, and there is more crime being committed, than officers are being employed. What if one day my kids are harmed for an arrest I made? What if I hurt someone by accident and they want to hurt me by getting my kids? As a cop you learn you can't protect someone 24/7. You literally have to have faith and keep going. Even though I am supposed to uphold the law it seems like people break it even more when we are around, and they do the littlest things to try and tick us off. I wanted to protect people but, where my post is, not everyone likes the cops, it is like it's us against them. Although they may view it that way, it is not like that in my head, they are not my enemy. Once a family member has been traumatized by the police however, there is nothing you can do about it. I guess I would not trust me either. I always have a gun, but you learn that it is intended for safety. This deadly weapon has to be treated like your heart, I can't just always go showing it and putting it out there. The day I make the wrong decision or get scared, I can hurt someone; shit I can lose my kids. My life is not easy being a cop, a woman at that. People will test you. They think you cannot back yourself and they might be stronger than me but, I am well trained, even though they just see a woman. One of the happiest moments was when I lost weight in training. I felt good about myself but after sitting and riding around in the car, I gained a lot. I do not know if I can run that far, or that fast; maybe a bad guy will get away.

That is one of my worst thoughts ever. This is being a woman cop in America, one of the most dangerous and courageous jobs in the world. The reality check was that all the things I thought to be true weren't, and it isn't safer. My kids have more problems than usual, but I make it work because I am a part of the NYPD, the proud family."

Interviewer: "Wow what an amazing point of view. I agree that people might want to take advantage because you are a woman. Being a woman in a police officer uniform is not easy, that is why it is good to remind yourself of the truth of what is in front of you, and not to be oblivious. It's good to keep your head on your shoulders even though you are the boys in blue. I would like to say I appreciate you for putting your life on the line every day. I appreciate you for coming to speak with me and sharing your truth, sharing your experience with having a reality check in a 'fake reality'."

Interview 4

Interviewer: "Hey, how are you? can you tell us a little about yourself, Have you ever caught yourself living in a fake reality? If so, can you tell us a little about that time.

Interviewee 4: "Growing up I always played doll house, my biggest dream was to start a family. I wanted to live as I played. I remember seeing my parents be so happy and joyful. They ate together, prayed together, even learned and laughed together. It was like watching my doll house dreams in real life. I never knew if they disagreed. They always kept their conversations behind closed doors. It was never where we could hear them or see them. They never disagreed in front of me, I loved it. I said to myself that when it is time for me to get married, I'm going to have kids, my husband will take care of us, and our family would never fight. I wanted that so bad that I convinced myself I had it when I really did not. I was really a single mother with a bad roommate."

Interviewer: I'm sorry, can you elaborate on what you meant by roommate? Also, is this the time you realized you lived in a fake reality?"

Interviewee 4: "Mm, where can I start? So, the father of my children does not help me with anything, he lays around the house always asking, always taking, never fully giving. It is annoying to feel like you have to carry everything on your back. It is uncomfortable to feel like if you did not work today then that is it, both you and your kids go hungry. I come home and he wants me to cook after a long day of me working. We argue in front of our kids! "What am I showing my girls?" I ask myself. "I did not learn this, am I teaching them to accept less?" But it is their dad. All I know is that I had kids before I got married. He didn't have the same respect my father did for my mother. We were not always laughing, and it was not always good. Sometimes he ate out without us. Even though he brought food back, I said to myself "what kind of family man does that?" It was nothing like when I played house in my doll house. It was confusion, anger, pain, it was unbearable. Everything was always in the open and we had neighbors in our business. Our supposed to be private life was a television show that aired every time I got home. I was drained. I realized that relationships are not easy, and no one is perfect. My parents played their part in raising us well, but it sure makes me think of what happened behind those closed doors, especially if I'm dealing with what I'm dealing with. But, nevertheless, I wasn't getting the treatment I deserved. I wasn't even being considered. I couldn't believe most of the things that happened. Our children are the ones who take the biggest hit. If we are not synced and one with our love, how can they be? So, you see why that's my roommate? Sometimes when he's sleeping, I just want to slap him upside his head, but I don't 'cause I know that would be another thing to fight about."

Interviewer: "It is unfortunate to hear how intense your reality check in a fake reality is. Children make toxicity harder to break; especially if they don't understand what's going on. That's why you should stay strong. It is hard to change when others are stuck in a way, but you must break through for a better living situation. You are fortunate enough to see the fake reality. So, you have a chance to change it for the better. You can break toxic."

Now that we have the concept of what a reality check is in a fake reality, do you see that in all realities what you deem as perfect can be different, or what you tell yourself about someone can harm you knowing the underlying truth? Toxicity comes from you wanting unneeded negativity or being accustomed to it. In reality that contributes to the dysfunctional life that you may be trying to escape. I am not saying it is easy because it is not, but the first step is understanding yourself.

8

Monitoring Your Feelings

Impulsiveness is the lack of monitoring your mood change. Take notes on how you feel around the energy you want to get away from. For example, if you are with someone you deem as toxic, change how you act around them, make sure they are limited to a few decisions around you. This way if there is collateral it is kept at bare minimum. When it comes to lightening the load of toxicity you must decide what the load is. What you get is not what you usually perceive.

You should know when to give yourself a break from a thought process, too much thinking is not always healthy. It's okay to give yourself a break. The brain is like a computer and even those machines take breaks. Although breaking toxic is already an intense transition for most humans, you should still slow the thought process down if it becomes overwhelming. Once you break open the doors of toxicity to see what the true issue is, anything can come out pouring if it is not managed the right way. If that happens it can cause emotional death.

I teach all humans to pull through. Pulling through doesn't mean you heal right away. People heal differently than other people. If you need to walk then you walk, maybe it works for you. The quarantine method is a great method to give yourself space. If you haven't done it, then try it. Pay attention to how you think all the time. Try to make sure the process does not kill you emotionally. Death of who you were is the goal to break toxicity. Tell yourself it is okay to walk away or not to respond. In life we are shown that it's not okay to walk away from toxicity. The real answer is, yes you can. Manners don't matter when it comes to your mental health, there is no proper way to walk away, as long as you start walking, it's fine. Don't stay there to torture yourself. It is also okay to respond in a way that limits or ends conversation. That is a great technique to use when you can foresee toxic behavior.

In this chapter I will be teaching you to avoid relationship toxicity. I will implant a different way of thinking, so it is easier for you to process what is actually going on. Use these techniques to master conversations while manipulating energy. This technique ultimately leaves you in power, you get to decide how it will end if you didn't decide how the conversation started.

Avoiding Relationship Toxicity

When you disagree with your partner you should take a step back. Asking your partner to speak more clearly can change a lot of outcomes. Most people if not all would like to be understood. Understanding that everyone's life experience is different is the key to handling situations. If you know your partners habits, then you shouldn't trigger their toxicity. It takes time to change, try to take a different route. Respond in a calm tone, use the unicorn effect to disable any negative thoughts that come to your mind.

Dealing with family isn't easy when it comes to toxicity. I find the truth is the best possible response to navigate through negative conversations. I also understand that everyone has their own truth. So, speak your piece. You must also learn to respect someone's else's thoughts. Let the toxicity go, healing is a universal medicine that we all need. If you have children just always remind yourself, they are children. It isn't an overnight 1-2-3 situation. If you want their toxicity to stop a different approach must be taken. When you're dealing with someone at work who sexualizes everything in my experience a straightforward response will suffice. You can't allow anyone to get away with small remarks that can lead to more toxicity. Break Toxicity by living by what you want, while being what you need.

In the sentences above I explained to you how to deescalate toxic situations by changing your response by keeping control over your feelings but also understanding the other person's point of view. Tighten up your words, make your responses impeccable. Break the habit of toxic behavior. Reminding yourself it is your space and your time; you can do and say what you want with it. Do not allow others to invade your space mentally and bring in their toxicity. The truth of the matter is, that you are just allowing your toxic to dance with theirs. You must always remember the feelings you had before you started to learn how to break toxic. Use it as a mental reference sheet to thyself. Remember the feelings you get when you have control over the toxic situation. Love it, become an addict of peace. If you ever forget what happened that's okay. Just don't forget how you felt. Energy never dies.

9

Knowing When and How

Knowing when toxic is taking over is vital, you cannot properly handle a problem until you are able to recognize that there is one. It is important to catch toxic traits and behaviors before they get out of hand. A problem that is not properly handled can lead to a toxic take over. When toxicity has taken over, it will feel as if your life's energy is being drained from what will feel like your soul. A toxic takeover comes with so many signs and symptoms. I like to think of it as a virus that you have allowed to invade your body.

You will experience intense emotions varying from anger, jealousy, rage, hatred, sadness, depression, envy, self-pity, and even suicide. You may even experience happiness, love, over confidence, and self-acceptance. The emotional roller coasters are some of the hefty signs that the virus is destroying you from the inside out. You're probably already asking yourself how does happiness and self-acceptance sound toxic? I will be answering that shortly. Symptoms may also include a blinded ego, over sought stress, and what I like to call, self-suffering syndrome. A blinded ego is the result of suppressing the cause of these emotions, and when you begin living in a dishonest way with not only yourself but the world, you become willfully blind to the toxicity that you are encountering.

Your ego then builds a shell composed of trigger events and the emotional responses to them. Living through this toxicity drives you a little crazy in fact, it might guide you through the reality that we all turn a blind eye to; that's the reality that lives on around you. You should now understand why experiencing happiness, love or self-acceptance when in this stage can be a problem. These emotions are taking place from only what your mind is processing while being blinded by your egos created shell. When living blinded, reality is unable to be seen. It is difficult to understand what is clearly happening in front of your eyes. This works the same way for all the listed emotions and symptoms you may experience. You have merely suppressed all that is toxic in or around you at the cost of, what you think is your comfort zone in life. When you have allowed yourself to become comfortable functioning in this deep and toxic environment you must do more work to save yourself. A blinded ego becomes a blinded life.

Think back to a toxic relationship you were in. Maybe you're still in it. Can you remember the first sign of sickness your conscious tried to send to your body? I chose the word conscious so that you understand that you are aware of the moment when something toxic is in your presence. That allows you to choose whether you allow it in or not. Whatever form it may be in, the sooner you realize the truth, the closer you can get to your true healing. Living comfortably suppressed in a shell of toxicity will not allow you to live in the 'now'. You will find that time and time again you are in a repetitive vortex of events.

Allowing yourself to be free is to kill everything you know about yourself. It has to be the death of you, the toxic you, the you that holds yourself back, the you that destroys your youth with a minuscule way of thinking. You must not fight the path that can help you change. You shouldn't be scared of the you that you know is there. Growth is inevitable. Once you plant a seed you cannot stop the growth unless you dig it back up. Your environment is always changing and what you see and learn can be unlearned once you know how to see toxicity. This will also always be a given gift. It is like once you know how to read, it becomes automatic. Try to look at this page without reading it. Impossible right!? Your brain just does it. If you leave the seed planted outside to experience the world as it is, it will grow through the terrain and become what it is supposed to be. The experiences do not get removed from the seed. Once it is planted from rain to snow, the seed grows.

From memory to mistakes our minds won't forget and they too, GROW.

Although it is inevitable, having a moat around your soul is not the best option; you must be able to allow things to flow through you. It is a big challenge; therefore, you must always see yourself as a conductor. You must allow yourself to live how you would, not how someone else would like you to. We are at a point in this book where you take the lessons you've learned and practice. No one person does something and becomes a pro at it overnight. In the words of the late great Kobe Bryant "great things come from hard work and perseverance, no excuses."

If you want to be better, you continue to push through because being free of toxicity comes with no excuses, it comes with putting yourself first! You have to strive for that inner peace, inner freedom. Changing your habits is essential to becoming successful in breaking toxic. Even if it is a struggle to change your mind because of what has been embedded there for so long, think of changing your habit as a second person in your life to help you do what you need to live. It is a cheat code for life to be honest. This is very important. If your mind cannot change, your habits will remain the same and continue to kill you.

I used to wake up late every day. I was really tired of being late so what I did was buy alarm clocks and placed them on each side of the bed. Every day I would wake up at 4:00 am to shut off the alarm clocks. Sometimes I would fall back asleep but over time it became a natural awakening. Even when the battery died in the alarm clock I would still wake up. I have built a habit that could help me destroy my old habits. Even if your mind doesn't change right away. Your decision to change your habits will play a big role in becoming free. It kills the toxic version of you when you do it repetitively; filling up your schedule with reachable goals, you can achieve a lot.

We all have that day of "ugh" in our lives. We wake up just not feeling ourselves or the world we live in. Well, let me make this clear, get over yourself, because laying in defeat is also a toxic trait that needs to be destroyed. In life you can either be the problem or create a solution, it's really up to what you desire. Take me for example, I wanted to write this book to help others with their toxicity and I desired to do so. Therefore, I used everything in my power to make this happen, even on my worst days, I wrote. When it seemed like the world was ending, I wrote. When I was sad, I wrote. When I didn't have the mindset of a writer, I wrote. My point is I decided to continue and face what was going on in life head on, while being head strong. If you completely shut down, don't panic. It is okay to be quiet for a few days, just do not allow those days to become your worst enemy. Understand under those conditions you are the only opponent in site. Most people start harming their selves by speaking negative to oneself, most beings look back into their minds and see the worst rather than seeing a solution.

Most people are not okay but put on a poker face to have the illusion of togetherness. That act is a broad statement of not breaking toxic. You must go the opposite way and, in the darkness, speak light. Remember darkness is the original light. So, in solitude where there is nothing, anything can be created. Clear your mind and make your demons your puppets and take over your life.

Your rebirth is needed more for the soul. You will probably go through all stages from depression to happiness. When you come out of that, you must choose who you would like to be. You must choose the warrior that you have inside. Do not choose the person that doubted themselves, that form of you must die for you to truly be alive.

Committing to the Life You Want

What is commitment? If you go on the internet you can find that commitment means "the state or quality of being dedicated to a cause or an activity." Nevertheless, if you're going by what you live by, then you should really ask yourself what this word means to you. I can tell you what commitment means to me. Commitment is a conscious choice made by the soul; fully surrendering yourself to what you believe despite the obstacles you may face. Commitment to me is freedom by sacrifice. Sacrificing the things, you want for the things you need. Commitment is never giving into the toxic you. For you to break toxic you MUST COMMIT, DO IT FOR YOUR-SELF, for your future goals, for your future happiness, do it to be free. Who wants to live in a toxic environment? No one! We are so accustomed to living in bad situations where we often forget that we do not have to. We think we do due to a systemic way of living. I guarantee if someone were in a bad situation that they fully understood was bad for them that they would want to leave.

The techniques you have learned here equip you to be your own technician. Once you commit to yourself getting out of a toxic relationship or situation is right around the corner. Do you want to be a person of great interest for corporations? Then commit. Do You want to be a great baseball player? Then commit! If you want the life you saw on television, then commit! Tyler Perry is a great example of commitment. When he lost "everything" he did not lose sight of his dreams. Life filled with toxicity and he committed. He committed to writing his plays. Therefore, he committed to himself. Tyler Perry lived out of his car for 3 months and wrote more. He was committed to the change he wanted, and he went for it. He got it. In order to change your life, you must commit. From the alarm clocks waking me up, to meditation, you must commit. Commit to becoming a better you for you.

What is your biggest priority? I know that is a funny question, there are so many important things out there to choose from in your life. The greatest choice you can make is choosing yourself. If you are not well no one is. I truly feel that if you're not in the right state of mind that nothing will be right. No one will be right; it will always be difficult if you are not fully functioning at your highest potential that you can. When you know you can give 100 percent, but you give ninety-nine and wonder why you are not getting the results you want, it isn't because of anyone but yourself. No one is coming to save you. You have to do it yourself.

You should always observe, Observing is the better route than reacting or staying in the cycle. I observe everything. You can learn from an ant as much as you can learn from an elephant. Everything we see has a unique algorithm which helps us learn as we see. We even learn while we sleep. The body itself is a learning machine, for example, what is comfier versus what is not. Our muscles combined with our lack of comfort carry's energy through our body and then we move.

Energy is real pay attention to what you feel. Never be obsessed with just a thought. Never allow it to distract you from what you have control over. The right thing to do is to let it out. Go for a walk by the water or go do karaoke. Breaking toxic is a process it will not be done in a day, but it will change your life in the long run.

Take a second to close your eyes and take 10 deep breaths. Think of all the toxicity you have built in you. Think of a place you would like to be, any place. Now imagine the toxicity being a baseball. Take it and throw it as far as you can. If you imagine being by a lake, throw it into the lake. If you imagine being in the desert, throw it into the sand away from you. Change is okay. Sometimes we hold on to things that we are used to but most of the time it would be better for us to push that negativity out and let the positivity in. Change is inevitable so you must accept that and live!

We all grow up being programmed from television shows as well as our family's behaviors. Although I mainly focus on the programs that instilled toxicity in our lives, there are also programs that have taught us good as well. You have to decide what your "happy" is. What is it that you were shown in this world that makes up happiness to you? Asking yourself this is a good technique to actually making yourself happy. Finding your true happiness and breaking toxic is to be found within you, it is there. This technique is a step closer to making yourself happy. Finding your true happiness is within you. Breaking toxic is there.

II

❧

Letting Go | Draw a Picture

The scariest choice is to let go. Letting go is the death of what you used to know. It's the feeling you get in the pit of your stomach, the roller coaster drops; it is regret, pain or even worst the Stockholm syndrome. We don't know how to let go; we think everything has to be an endless marathon. We blame ourselves for someone else's choices while we have been denying ourselves our truth. The key is us. Sometimes we think that we are not ready for the next step even though a step further is a step away from toxicity. Any steps we take are most likely not in our comfort zone. Comfortability should not exist until you break toxicity. Within every step you take, something changes. Once you learn what you want, you start to feel better knowing that it is okay to let go of anything that is not good for you.

Letting go of being toxic is letting go of an addiction. The addiction is the worst half of you. You should know that it is okay to feel sorrow from a past situation but important to remember it is in the past and cannot coexist with the you that you are now. It is not happening anymore, at least not in the realm you are living in. When you get past something you shouldn't go backwards to try and relearn the struggle when you have already dealt with it. Understand, healing is a crucial part of breaking toxic. In order to break away from toxicity you must know that recovery can last as long as you need it to. Don't go back to being an addict and stay away from what's breaking you down or making you relapse.

Breaking toxic is a lifestyle that must be practiced every day. The mind is a muscle that you use nonstop. Think of breaking toxic as your mind's new workout regimen. When you realize there will always be a struggle between the human heart and mind, Positive Repetitiveness is the cure. No matter what we do, if toxicity is inside of us, there will always be a struggle between the mind and the heart. It is amazing that we can have two main organs functioning on different levels. To have these organs (heart and brain) function the same is to have the strength of will. To have them move as one, like our bodies with our souls, is the power of freedom.

Being positive when you feel like your heart is torn is the best way to go. Using positivity towards your needs is the name of the game. If you spend your time trying to be positive for someone else's needs, then that really isn't positivity directed towards your needs.

What do you say to help yourself let go of the toxicity? Repeat after me. Say this affirmation 10 times each day every time you feel the toxic energy in your life or, see your traits of toxicity coming on due to a relapse,

> "I have already changed. I love myself for who I became and for who I was. I am not a stagnant person. My heart is pure. Breaking toxic is a lifestyle. I love myself and that is where it starts, everything is going to be okay, maktub. I chose myself and that is okay. I am living the life I want. I love the process. I love life."

After that sit back and take it in. You spoke your life and new energy into existence.

12

LYF

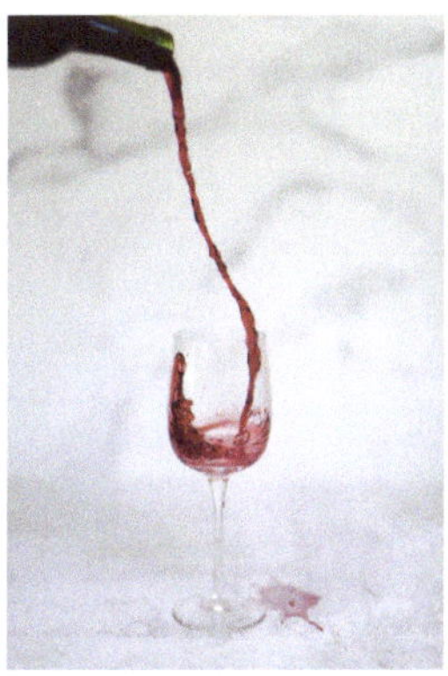

I almost gave up on myself. I found every pain that was hidden beneath my surface and discovered new growth from things I buried. It was like being connected to a connection that I didn't want there anymore. That is what I told myself; it was easier to say that than to be honest. I buried the most hurtful situations. Key word, buried. I did not face them after experiencing life's painful trials. I ran. I was shocked at how years after the experiences, the decisions I make every day were being affected in ways that I thought they couldn't. What you bury inside of you can grow. Nature and the spirit are everlasting so you cannot run from what you bury for forever.

Reevaluating yourself is the best thing to do. Sometimes hearing about yourself from a close friend or even an ex-partner after breaking toxic or while going through the process, is good. If you can calm your mind and listen to what is being said, you'll be able to see the damage that has been done. You think, "how could I be that person to you?" When you are not being true to yourself you become everything, you don't want to be, just for temporary relief. That is the worst part of being toxic, knowing that it starts from yourself. Knowing that you cannot stop someone from being who they are, but you can stop yourself from being around them. However, we usually do not stop, we lack the strength to separate because we deem it as a weakness. Sometimes separation is for the best, and not for the other person but, for you. I'm pretty sure there are a lot of critics that have an idea of how the Mona Lisa should have been painted. I'm sure a lot of artist came and said they could do it better. Once you paint a picture for the whole world to see, good or bad, the world now knows you for this painting. Similarly, once you have shown a person a version of you, good or bad, people now remember you as that person or what they might have interpreted as you. Knowing this, you have to continue to paint. You are capable of creating more art in this world, with an opportunity each time to decide on what is it that would make the next one better. You cannot let anyone decide for you what your best picture is. Even if you showed someone that you were a monster, do not allow that image to be where you end. Loving yourself first is like recovery and for anyone that understands what recovery is, you know it is something that we all need. We can be in re-covery for years because it is all about the that may be needed for you to heal. Once you are in recovery however, that does not mean it's okay to go back and do the same thing that in-jured you. That's where breaking toxic is a necessity. You must recover inside and out. You must know toxic starts from what you accept as acceptable. It's okay to say I'm not going to that party tonight. It does not make you a bad friend. It is okay to say no, I am not doing what we have always done. It doesn't make you a person who doesn't care. It is okay to sit back and enjoy some you time. It doesn't make you a selfish person. And it is also okay to refuse to deal with someone else's issues, especially if you do not have your own under control. Lov-ing yourself has been taught selfishly to us, in a way that has shown us to neglect others. However, genuinely loving your-self first actually provides you with the completely opposite effect.

If you can love yourself more, you can give more love to other people. If you understand yourself more, you will be able to understand other people better. Allowing yourself to live as who you are, who you were, and who you are becom-ing can be the most fulfilling achievement you will ever do for yourself. Loving yourself is not throwing yourself into talking to someone new right after a breakup. It is not devouring all of the normal distractions, whatever may be the distraction, in one week in attempt to make yourself feel better. Because guess what? In the end when your body stops and when your mind is tired, It's likely you brought the old toxic relation-ship into the next one and made more decisions in that binge week that have hindered you or maybe even injured you in the process.

Ever heard the saying what is done in the light comes to the dark. Guess what? That is bullshit when talking about yourself. What's done in the dark is already in the light, we just choose to ignore it. However, just because you change the light settings of a room does not mean the object in the room changes. You physically must go in there and deal with what you left behind, or you must remove it. This way, you'll always know what is in there. This is why loving yourself first is so important because, if you don't love yourself on your own, you'll lack the love you desire to have in your relationships. The lack of love will form as a weapon against you.

Again, we are taught loving yourself first is selfish, however, true self love, for better or for worse, allows you work on yourself before you seek acceptance and attention from anywhere or anyone else. Unlearn and relearn. It is a gift to have another chance at loving yourself. Even in a workplace loving yourself is okay. Work teaches us to work in teams, but when you start to do more for the team and not focus on the work you were assigned to complete as an individual, that becomes an issue.

The boss will say okay that is good you did that with the team but, what about your work? That is good you did that for him/her but, what about you? You should model your self-love work the same way.

The "don'ts" of loving yourself:

1. Do not move on too quickly from any relationship to the next, good or bad, if you still have not found yourself. Remember that you need time and distance from a toxic relationship.
2. Don't choose things that make you feel at ease because you want to be distracted. Reminder: the distraction is just a high for the moment but, forced highs do not last forever, only natural ones do.
3. If loving yourself costs you the people you care about then that is okay because you forgot about the person you should care about the most, and that is you.

Losing opportunities or people is a part of living and should be looked at not as a loss, but as a new opportunity to grow. Even a caterpillar becomes a butterfly. When the caterpillar is experiencing this change there is the possibility it might know what to anticipate, it might have had some guidance on what is to come from seeing other caterpillar's; however, if the caterpillar has never actually experienced the change itself, then it still has some understanding it may need to experience from the change that is now here.

Because the caterpillar took time to love itself and grow itself it was able to adapt to become a better version. Butterflies do not fly around caterpillars because they cannot fly but they do soar high in the sky with new butterflies. That's also part of loving yourself, even when you felt like you left behind a part of you, you are able to enjoy the growth and transition into something new. There is a whole new part to explore and love because we never take time to explore the parts of us now that we overlook daily. Overlooking yourself allows toxicity to take place because if you do not know you're worth a million dollars anyone can tell you you're a dollar and you may begin to believe them. You have to love yourself the way you know you deserve.

LYF. I feel that we as people should know that life is a gateway to a powerful gift. We all have the ability to achieve this gift, have this gift become our own, and that gift is LOVE. In order to really understand that, you must know self-love is the reflection in all love. How you love yourself is how you will eventually love the world and if you are short on love most likely a toxic serum is around the corner.

It takes all of you to love yourself. It takes the parts you try to forget, and it takes a consistent positive reminder to drive out the negative. It takes tears, it takes forgiveness, it takes allowance, it takes the strength, and the inside light to shine for you to love yourself first and consistently. It is one of the hardest uphill battles. The goal is to get to the top of your hill, whatever you might imagine the top to be. It is your hill, your happiness, your freedom your space of breaking toxicity. Keep climbing but do not ever forget to love the travels because that is a part of who you are as well, the little things that matter should not be overlooked. I used to be upset about certain attire that I wore but then I realized I had a body to wear it on. That sounds so simple, but it is the little things that are the bigger pictures that we overlook. I used to complain about not having all the right socks, but I have feet and that is the little thing we overlook.

Never ever put yourself in a corner where you feel like you have nothing to love about yourself. Find it, say it, and go upwards from there because only your words will break the toxic in you. Only your thoughts will make you better. Loving every part of you is loving yourself first. Perfect does exist. Perfect is imperfections, for that's perfection at its greatest. No place you go will be perfect, no one you speak to will have all the knowledge, and no one in the world leaves their toxic behavior fully behind. Inside of you are where the answers resonate. Perfect is perspective and if you can change your mind on other subjects in the world, you can change yourself into a perfect being of nontoxic behavior. Again, perfection is perspective. You must not live using the world's definition of perfection but live your perfection.

13

Living in the new you

At this point in breaking toxic, you have realized that everything is based on you. Yes, I said it again, everything is based on you. No one else can change what's here or what's to come. When we grow, things change it's in your best interest to accept that. Accept what you always wanted and what you practiced for, and do not allow anyone to make your peace a crime. Take what you learned and show the world that altering your mind with your energy sets the stage ahead for a life with little to no toxicity. Show yourself repeatedly that anything can be achieved. Take what you learned and leave toxic-

74

ity behind. Develop goals, take trips, be everything you know you can be. Control toxic energy because you know it well.

Remember every time is not perfect but strive for the best outcome, and be the self you always wanted to be, toxic free.

Remember to apply all that you know.

Reread if you must.

Take notes if you must.

Speak out loud if you must.

Let the inner light shine because it never truly dims.

Take your last toxic situation and create a space where it went how you wanted it to go and treat new situations like that.

Apply what you learned and then everything else around you will follow.

What I Learned

What I learned about humanity through the eyes of toxicity and healing is that we all have the tendency to dwell in our past, even if it's for a little while. It shows through our energy in an enormous way. The pressure of the world creates an invisible ball of toxicity, because we are trained from birth what we are supposed to be like. The environment you live in and the people you grow up around have a greater part to play in this. Once you start growing and learning this world, what was embedded in you will expand and the "facts" and opinions you once thought you knew will transform and merge into a different level of awareness. If you happen to realize what is going on then you are in the stage of unlearning and relearning and that is a killer stage of life. To think that everything you once knew could be wrong or maybe it isn't right for you just because it may be right for someone else. You see breaking toxic is bigger than human relationships, it is bigger than only your personal energy or agenda. It's a world pandemic. The fact that we stay stuck because our minds are bind to sources that use fear mongering as a weapon; the weapons being another person's mind, thought process or their strong opinion that you might trust.

You can trust someone and that does not mean they are not toxic, and it doesn't mean they are healed; most of us are broken. We start by ignoring it and not addressing the issue of life. The only obstacle that is stopping you from understanding all your issues, is you. The human in the mirror is the human with the key. The key to a way of thinking that can set you free. Free from boundaries that enable the act of toxicity. It is time now to give yourself what you need, and that is to break through the toxic traits. Fight against it, anything worth having doesn't come easy. Follow through with the process, while challenging everything you knew. Being able to get up and change is the best feeling in the world and if you fall it's okay, we didn't learn how to walk in a day. Therefore, it will take practice and determination. All goals can be reached through persistence. Break free! Live better! Love life!

More from the Author

Instagram @tonydflash

Published Books

NINE BY,
Tony D Flash

Tony D Flash Owner of,
www.flashsupplementsllc.com
Instagram @flashsupplementsllc

"Where your journey meets nature."
A company that provides natural herbal remedies to help aide the body in healing, weight loss, weight gain and mental focus.

Tony D Flash Owner of,
www.thecheapestthingsllc.com
"The Best Product for Me, At the Best Price It Could Be!"
-The Cheapest Things LLC
Also known as,
TCT.
A company that strives on giving their customers a chance. With everything at such an affordable price, you're able to save when you shop with us so that you can put more money aside for your goals.

www.ingramcontent.com/pod-product-compliance
Lightning Source LLC
Chambersburg PA
CBHW041222050726
47599CB00001B/33